37 Houseplants Even You Can't Kill

37 Houseplants

Even You

Can't Kill

MARY KATE HOGAN

Sterling Publishing Company

A John Boswell Associates Book

Design by Nan Jernigan

**Library of Congress
Cataloging-in-Publication Data Available**

2 4 6 8 10 9 7 5 3 1

Published by Sterling Publishing Co., Inc.
387 Park Avenue South, New York, NY 10016
© 2006 by Sterling Publishing Co., Inc.

Distributed in Canada by Sterling Publishing
c/o Canadian Manda Group, 165 Dufferin Street
Toronto, Ontario, Canada M6K 3H6
Distributed in the United Kingdom by GMC Distribution Services
Castle Place, 166 High Street, Lewes, East Sussex, England BN7 1XU
Distributed in Australia by Capricorn Link (Australia) Pty. Ltd.
P.O. Box 704, Windsor, NSW 2756, Australia

Sterling ISBN-13: 978-1-4027-4089-3
ISBN-10: 1-4027-4089-1

For information about custom editions, special
sales, premium and corporate purchases, please contact
Sterling Special Sales Department at 800-805-5489
or specialsales@sterlingpub.com.

Contents

Introduction   ix

The Basics

Let There Be Light   1
Water, Water Everywhere—But Not Too   4
    Much to Drink
Find a Home Sweet Home   7
Feed Me!   11
    The facts on fertilizer
Cheat Sheet: 14
    Tricks of the trade for beautiful plants
Grow Forth and Multiply   17
Plant Problem Solvers   20
Great Ways to Display   25

Foliage Plants

Arrowhead Plant	30
Baby's Tears	32
Cast-Iron Plant	34
Century Plant	36
Chinese Evergreen	38
Corn Plant	40
Dumb Cane	42
Dwarf Schefflera	44
English Ivy	46
Fatsia	48
Heart Ivy	50
Jade Plant	52
Janet Craig	54
Lacy-Tree Philodendron	56
Lady Palm	58
Medicine Plant or Aloe Vera	60
Parlor Palm	62
Ponytail Palm	64
Pothos	66
Prayer Plant	68
Rosemary	70
Rubber Tree	72
Screw Pine	74
Southern Yew	76
Snake Plant	78
Spider Plant	80
Table Fern	82
Wandering Jew	84

Flowering Plants

African Violet 88
Amaryllis 90
Clivia 92
Dancing Ladies 94
Geranium 96
Kalanchoe 98
Peace Lily 100

Cacti

Christmas Cactus 104
Cactus 106

Quick Reference

When a Plant's Past Its Prime 109

Photo Credits 111
Acknowledgments 113
Index 115

Introduction

*e*ver get the impression that some people were born with a
magical talent for growing houseplants—and you're simply
not one of them? Here's a little secret: Success has less to do with
the person and more to do with the plant. You are not missing
some mysterious green gene! Sure, it's easy to feel guilty when the
leaves on your ficus tree start to drop off in droves or your prayer
plant stops praying. Okay, the fact that you left them in a dark
corner and forgot to water them for months probably didn't help.
But it's time to cut yourself some slack.

If your life is hectic (and whose isn't?) and you still want to fill your home with foliage, you just have to pick the right plants—namely, the ones that will hold their own in the face of minimal TLC. With that in mind, this book points you to the easygoing side of the garden center: thirty-seven tough cookies that won't kick the bucket if you miss a watering or two. Do you occasionally forget you even own plants? Have you been known to utter "Honey, what's that green thing behind the couch?" Well, there's more than one here that will work for you. These thirty-seven generous houseplants give so much—extra oxygen, gorgeous leaves, lively flowers—while asking so little in return.

When you finally turn your attention to your all-natural pals, they often reward you with new buds or leaves. And the notion that you played some small role in producing this greenery can be oddly satisfying. Friends and family may compliment you on the verdant additions to your decor. Just smile graciously. It's okay to pride yourself on your gardening prowess, even if that only means you're savvy at selection.

The easiest way to find the plants described in this book is to ask for them by their common names. But I've also provided the botanical names because many have more than one moniker. For instance, the snake plant and mother-in-law's tongue are the same thing. You get the idea: it's one prickly, but almost indestructible, plant. Likewise, the Southern yew is also known as the Buddhist pine; Chinese evergreen is often called the pewter plant; and the list goes on. So if the folks at your local plant center seem confused by your request (let's hope they don't), try the botanical name instead.

While the thirty-seven low-maintenance beauties in this book are forgiving by nature, they won't tolerate apathy forever. Ignore them for too long, and eventually they take the hint. Fortunately, all they really require, for the most part, are three essential elements: sunlight, water, and a decent spot to spread their roots. The following chapter on basic care will tell you everything you need to know to make room for more green in your life.

The Basics

Let There Be Light

*e*very plant needs a little sunshine, some more than others. Light is essential because plants convert it into the energy they need to grow and flower. There are several in this book that can survive in fluorescent light alone. But, ideally, you should place most plants within five or six feet of a window, but not so close that the leaves or flowers touch the pane—very cold temperatures or scorching sun can damage the greenery. Set them about a foot back from the glass.

Do some window shopping.

Where you position your plants (i.e., a sunny or shady window) can have everything to do with whether they'll thrive. Which exposure is most hospitable to houseplants? That depends on the plant—and the window. Some houses have trees and awnings blocking the light. And if you live in an apartment, the sunlight may be hindered by the high-rise next door. But, in general, a northern-facing window gets the least amount of sun. That doesn't mean it's a bad locale: Plenty of the low-light-tolerant plants in this book will do just fine there. An east- or west-facing window gets a medium amount of light (though western sun is more powerful). The strongest sun is found in a southern window. For some plants, especially in the hot summer months, this light can be too intense.

How to choose the right window for each plant? I'll give you the precise recommendations under each of the plant listings. But if you know that your home has few sunny windows, or you're just looking for something to brighten up a dreary office, check out the quick list "Plants that love low light" on p. 10.

Though the plants in this book are gems at adapting to different locales, don't assume that you can keep the same plant in the same spot year-round. When the sun's intense, in early July for instance, you may need to provide some plants with a bit more shelter. Likewise, in the colder months when outside light is dim, you may want to find them a brighter space to rest.

Take geography into account.

Of course, your experience with houseplants will be different if you live in a warm, sunny climate, like Florida or Southern

California, versus a colder zone that gets less light in the winter, like New England, the Midwest, or the Plains states. If you live in the South—lucky you, you get more light—all of the advice here still applies, but you may need to be even more careful about shielding houseplants from the scorching summer sun. Likewise, you may not need to move your plants to where they'll get extra light in the winter. Many of the tropical varieties that can only grow indoors in the north will flourish outside, year-round in a southern zone.

As a rule of thumb, most flowering houseplants need more light than foliage plants. All plants are phototropic, which simply means they grow toward the light. If you notice that all of the leaves are reaching out in one direction, rotate the plant and it will even itself out. And if the plant is constantly lopsided, take this as a sign that your friend needs a sunnier vista.

Water, Water Everywhere—
But Not Too Much to Drink

*t*he second essential ingredient in keeping plants alive is H_2O. I wish I could tell you to water just once a week and be done with it. But how often you water will depend on a few details: the size of the pot, what the pot is made of, what season it is, etc. Until you get to know your plants and develop a regular schedule, the best way to determine whether your friend is thirsty is to get your hands a little dirty.

Does your plant need water? Three ways to tell.

Try this test: Stick your finger about an inch into the soil. If the soil seems dry (it may crumble right off your fingertip), give the plant a drink. If it feels moist, don't water. Another easy water-check that won't mess up manicured nails: Poke a pencil into the potting mix. If it comes up clean, you know the soil's parched and it's time to water. If there are pieces of dirt stuck to the pencil, hold off on watering. A third way to tell whether your plant needs water is to pick up the plastic pot. If the container feels very light in weight, you know the soil's dried out and the plant's craving some liquid.

Less can be more. One of the main reasons plants are sent to an early grave is overwatering—*not* blatant neglect. I know I've been guilty of this. About a year ago, I realized that for weeks I hadn't looked at (much less watered) the rubber plant in my office. So instead of just giving it a quick drink, I drenched the poor thing repeatedly, hoping to revive it. More was not the answer! My old survivor started losing leaves within days. Fortunately, I recognized the error of my ways—or maybe I just got distracted—and backed off a bit. And today this amazing plant lives on.

Water by the calendar.

You'll find that many plants need more water during their active growing seasons (typically, the warmer months) and less water during the winter. While the plants are resting or growing at a slower pace, they simply don't need as much. Some of the hassle-free houseplants on the list can go without any water for more than a month at a time during the cold season. But on the pages that follow, you can read the specific guidelines for each plant.

Hold the cold H_2O.

Always water with tepid, room-temperature H_2O. Why? Most houseplants are native to the tropics; once upon a time, all of their water came from warm rain. If you suddenly douse them with frigid liquid, it's only going to stress them out. Think about it: Would you like to be forced into a 40-degree shower?
If you're looking for a goof-proof plant that can live without water for up to a month at a time, check out the quick list below for the ones in this book that act the most like camels.

Quick List

Plants that need the least water.

Every plant needs water to survive, but these are the camels of the plant world, the ones that will do the best with a forgetful owner.

Aloe/medicine plant
Cactus
Cast-iron plant
Century plant
Dracaenas (Janet Craig, striped, corn plant, etc.)
Jade plant
Ponytail palm
Rubber tree
Snake plant
Southern yew

Find a Home Sweet Home

i often feel the urge to buy new houseplants during the colder, grayer months of the year, when there's so little green outside. If you'd like to do the same, remember that plants are sensitive to cold air. Moving them from a warm, humid greenhouse to the chilly backseat of your car can shock their system. To start yourself off on the right foot, cover the plants in plastic wrap before you take them outside, then head for home as quickly as possible.

Once you get your houseplants inside, you'll want to pick a pot for each one—and not just any pot will do. In order for a plant to stay healthy, it must have drainage: a hole in the bottom of the container. Want to move your table fern from that tiny plastic tub into a decorative cachepot? Toss a few pebbles into the container before you pour in the potting mix; this will help the water drain more easily.

Clay vs. plastic.

Some gardeners favor the old-fashioned terracotta pots, but if you settle your plants in these classic containers, you'll need to water more often because the porous clay absorbs some of the moisture. If you're repotting in a clay pot, soak the container first; otherwise, it will quickly drain your plant of needed humidity. Plastic pots do the trick too. But you'll probably want to conceal them inside something more attractive (see "Great Ways to Display" on page 25); after all, if the plants don't help to decorate your home, what's the point?

Pick your potting mix.

Whichever container you choose, fill it with some good-quality potting mix, available at any garden center or nursery. Why pay for dirt when there's plenty in your backyard? The soil in your yard is often too dense for houseplants and could cause them to suffocate. Basic potting mix usually consists of peat moss, perlite, and composted bark; it's lighter in weight and drains more efficiently than dirt. If you have a compost pile, you can add some of that to the mix. Cacti and related plants called succulents require a sandier soil mix; you can buy this special cactus potting mix at a garden center.

When to repot.

If a plant is thriving in its home, you may think, Why mess with success? Why repot? Some plants are happier than others to live in one pot for years at a time. But suppose you were stuck in the same room, with the same four walls, for years. Eventually, you would develop cabin fever. The same is true for plants. They need new surroundings from time to time—a few scoops of fresh potting mix, a roomier container can work wonders.

Some experts say that it's a good practice to repot your plants every spring. This helps to encourage healthy growth. Sound like too much work? At the very least, take a sunny afternoon in spring to turn all of your pots upside down and check the roots. If they're poking out of the bottom, or if they appear completely cramped, the plant needs a new home. If you notice that you have to water more often than you used to, that's also a sign that it's probably time to upgrade your container. See "Plant Problem Solvers" on page 23 for tips on how to repot without damaging your plants.

A technique for tiding over.

So it's the middle of winter and you really don't feel like seeking out a new pot for your philodendron? Here's a trick to "freshen up" until you can do the job properly—outside, in the spring. Take a miniature trowel and remove some of the dirt around the sides of the plant. Replace it with some fresh potting mix on top. This will help to revive your faithful friend until you have time to change the container.

Quick List

Plants that love low light.

If your home is surrounded by trees and doesn't get loads of light, or you want a plant for an office that has only a tiny window, set yourself up for success by choosing one that can practically live in the dark.

Baby's tears
Cast-iron
Chinese evergreen
Dwarf schefflera and schefflera
Fatsia
Heart ivy
Janet Craig dracaena
Parlor palm
Pothos
Rubber tree plant

Feed Me!
The Facts on Fertilizer

*a*s a rule of thumb, flowering plants need more food than foliage plants. Though you should give most plants some fertilizer throughout the year, the warmer months (the active growing season) are the time when they need the most to eat. What exactly should you feed them?

For a safe bet, go with a liquid.

If you want an all-purpose fertilizer, fluid is the way to go. I'm sure many brands will do the job, but I've had good luck with liquid Miracle-Gro. This stuff lives up to its name and it's incredibly easy to use. You have to water the plants at some point anyway, so why not just squeeze a few drops of it into your H_2O? I've used it to bring cyclamen into a third round of blooming—not an easy task—and to keep plants at their healthiest. If you're watering once or twice a week, you could add liquid fertilizer every third watering. Or you can even use it just twice a month. A little goes a long way. To avoid overfertilizing (which can result in "burnt" leaves), use fewer drops per gallon of water.

Another brand that many experts swear by is Schultz Instant. It comes with a little medicine dropper, so it's also really easy to use. Just squirt a couple of drops into your watering can. A popular fertilizer that has a bit of a cult following is a brand called Algoflash, which is imported from Europe. This nontoxic, odorless liquid fertilizer is simple to use: Just add a capful to a gallon of water. Apparently, this environmentally friendly fertilizer is behind some of the Guinness World Records for largest plants and plants with the most blooms.

Skip the plant "spikes."

You'll see them at garden centers, advertised as the easiest way to fertilize. They seem simple—just stick them in the soil and they gradually release food. But they're not foolproof; you can accidentally hit the roots with a spike and this can seriously damage the plant.

Treat plants to seafood.

Many plants have a taste for something fishy. When you bring plants outside, during the warmer months, use a mixture of fish emulsion and liquid seaweed. The plants love it! It can be particularly helpful for your flowering varieties. Fishy fertilizers contain all kinds of healthy micronutrients. You could use this stuff indoors, but the smell might cause your family to leave home. The seafood-based fertilizer comes in a liquid form. All you need to do is pour a couple of teaspoons of each per gallon of water, following the directions on the package.

Never feed a "sick" plant.

Do not feed the plant when it it's in bad shape or it isn't actively growing. If you notice that many leaves have dropped off of a plant and it appears to be on its last legs, this is the worst possible time to introduce fertilizer: You could kill your plant. Imagine how you would feel if you were in bed with the flu and someone turned up to force-feed you a Thanksgiving feast. Well, plants are the same way. Wait until they're on the mend before offering them dinner.

Cheat Sheet
Tricks of the Trade for Beautiful Plants

*W*hat separates the green thumbs from the rest of us? Could be luck. Could be experience. Or it could be the help of certain "boosters." These very simple tools can help plants develop to their fullest—or at least look that way. With a little nudge, plants can turn out a few extra blooms and more abundant leaves. Once you've got the hang of just keeping plants alive, try these tools to promote lush foliage.

Plant shine spray.

Ever wonder why the plants in a nursery greenhouse look so shiny and appealing? Yes, plants love the warmth and humidity there, but there's another insider secret. Plant centers use a product called "plant shine," and you can buy this stuff and use it at home too. Spritz it directly onto plants' leaves to get rid of white spots and make them look healthy and shiny. Like a little gloss on your lips, it's a simple, quick pick-me-up. Don't abuse the spray, of course. It's not a cover-up for unhealthy leaves or insects, but it will make your greenery look extra gorgeous. One brand is the John Henry Company's Spring Leaf Shine. It's a great in-a-pinch solution when you don't have time to dust your plants and you're having people over. Note: You should use shine spray only on plants that have flat, smooth, relatively thick leaves, like scheffeleras, jade plants, fatsia, and kalanchoe. Don't spray this on fuzzier leaves (like African violet or streptocarpella) or thin, variegated leaves (like the arrowhead).

Humidifier.

Many houseplants have tropical origins and they much prefer a climate with moisture in the air; hence the invention of the green-house. If you place a humidifier in the room where you keep most of your houseplants, it will keep plants lush and leaves bright. It helps to ensure that your plants won't get stressed by the dry air. Plants love a setting of about 50 percent humidity, and these conditions are good for people too. Don't have a humidifier? One trick for the winter months is to group plants on a tray covered in pebbles and water.

Spray bottle.

Take an old spray bottle, clean it thoroughly, and fill with water and just a couple of drops of liquid fertilizer. Plant pros break out the spray bottle every few days, spritzing water directly onto the leaves of plants to keep them green and fresh.

Old-fashioned fan.

Once upon a time, before our houseplants were cultivated from the tropics, they lived in the jungle where the conditions were frequently changing and the breezes were plentiful. In your house the air is stagnant, and plants don't love that. They can actually develop more lush growth if you get the air around them moving. No need for a wind storm; just set the fan on low and oscillating at night.

Lazy gardener's food.

A product called HydraFeed is designed to make caring for your plants even more of a no-brainer. It contains liquid fertilizer, but is sold already premixed with water. It's tinted green (a positive sign), and you use it just as you would water. True, it takes a sluggish person to feel that walking over to the sink and filling up the watering can is too much trouble, but I'll own up to finding HydraFeed helpful for my office plants. When I was away on vacation, I asked a colleague to drop in on my amaryllis plants with a quick squirt of the stuff. When I returned, they were just about ready to bloom. Hand a bottle to your plant-sitter before your next trip, and you may come home to a greener space.

Grow Forth and Multiply

*O*nce you see how easy the plants in this book are to grow, you may decide you want to increase your brood. That's the great thing about many of these plants: If you follow one of these simple steps, they can multiply like rabbits. No need to spend more at the garden center. The technical term for the process is "propagation." There are whole books and classes dedicated to the subject, but here's all you really need to know when it comes to our beloved group. With a bit of trial and error, you'll be handing out baby plants to friends in no time. These are two basic methods for creating new "plantlings."

1) **Take a tip or leaf cutting.** If a plant has obvious branches with leaves on them, you can snip your way to new plants. Take your vinelike varieties and cut off at least a three-inch piece of the stem, with several leaves on it and, ideally a few nodes. (Nodes are little bumps of rapidly dividing tissue, found where a leaf attaches to a stem.) Dip the stem into rooting hormone—available at garden centers and nurseries— and plant it in the potting mix. You can also place stems in a glass of water and wait until you see roots forming at the tip before planting, but this process will result in slightly weaker roots. The plants that you can "clip and dip" include pothos, heart ivy, English ivy, arrowhead plant, wandering jew, and diffenbachia.

   With certain plants called succulents, all you need to create a new plant is a couple of leaves. Note: You can identify a succulent easily by pinching your nails into a leaf; if you get a little water on your fingers, you know it's a succulent. The technique works with African violet, kalanchoe, jade plant, and others. You pull the leaf from the stem, keeping the little tissue that attaches the leaf to the stem intact. Dip the stem end of the leaf into rooting hormone and put about one-third of the leaf into the soil. It will grow from there.

2) **Divide and conquer.** This is another straightforward process for propagation, though a slightly messier one. When you're repotting plants, you can actually separate them into two. One way to make this happen is to remove the plant from its pot, and try to gently pull on either side to split the roots and the foliage into two. With many species,

this can be a fairly hassle-free method for doubling your greenery. But some plants won't divide quite as easily. If the trial separation doesn't pan out, you have to cut through the roots. Sounds scary, but it does work. Division works well with ferns, rubber plant, Chinese evergreen, snake plant, cast-iron plant, Janet Craig dracaena, screw pine, and others like these.

Plant Problem Solvers

Problem #1: "Bugs are taking over."

*f*irst, you should know that pests are drawn to dusty leaves and soggy soil. If you keep your plants clean by picking off the dead leaves (I find this to be rather therapeutic) and dusting them from time to time, you should avoid bugs altogether. But if it's too late and you've got scales, mealy bugs, spider mites, or other pests, always take a natural, non-chemical approach first. Here's a four-step approach to getting rid of them. You may only need to follow step one, but if that doesn't work, move on to the next.

1) Place the plant in your kitchen sink and use the shower attachment to try to wash the bugs away. Be sure to check the back sides of the leaves and look for eggs tucked behind the stems. Note: With plants that are prone to pests (like ivy), this is a good weekly practice. Just bring your ivy pots over to the sink for a quick rinse to prevent an invasion of the plant snatchers.

2) If a shower doesn't eliminate the mites, dip a Q-tip or an old toothbrush into rubbing alcohol and dab it right onto the bugs. This should kill the bugs; rinse away as necessary.

3) The third line of defense is insecticidal soap. Try Safers brand and follow the directions on the package.

4) If soap doesn't do the trick, you can try one of several types of oils. Neem oil is good for stubborn insects like scales and spider mites. Also, orange oil and any citrus oil or a horticultural oil can get rid of the pests. The technique is to add two teaspoons to a quart and follow the instructions for spraying the plant.

A common mistake is to spray the plant and walk away, assuming that if you don't see any bugs, your work is done. The adult bugs are the visible ones, but you may not be able to notice the eggs that are still getting ready to hatch and the juvenile stage of insect may be there but not moving around. So keep an eye out every three or four days. If you've reached step four, just one application probably won't cut it.

Problem #2: "My plants have 'burnt' ends."

If the tips of the leaves on your plants are turning brown, you have what's called tip burn. This means the ends of the leaves are drying out. Some people see the brown ends and immediately assume the plant needs more water. This may or may not be the case. You get tip burn primarily as a result of low humidity or from the plants being caught in a hot or cold draft. To prevent and correct this, you need more moisture in the air, not necessarily in the pot. It's a good idea to keep a humidifier going in the room; set it until the room condition reaches about 50 percent humidity. An even easier way to boost the moisture is to group plants together.

Another possible cause of tip burn is salt buildup. If your plant is sitting in a wet saucer, that excess water can cause the salt in the soil (which comes from fertilizers) to leach to the top. Have you ever seen a clay pot that looked faded or white along the rim and on the sides? That's from salt. If the leaves touch the salt, they turn brown. The cure: Don't let your plant rest in water, and hold back a bit on your fertilizer. You may be overfeeding the plant.

Does your dracaena have brown tips? If it's not responding to the remedies I just listed, it may be reacting to the fluoride that's added to some cities' water. Dracaenas are particularly sensitive to fluoride. In that case, the solution is to use rainwater instead. The change in care should be enough to revive the leaf tips.

Problem #3: "My plant's normally pretty leaves have brown spots on them."

Leaf spotting is typically a sign of disease. Your plant may have a fungus or bacteria of some kind. Plants can become diseased when they're dirty or if you don't bother to snip off the dead flowers. Also, if you allow the leaves get too damp (beware of sloppy watering), this can make them susceptible to fungus.

If you notice a spot on just one or two leaves, simply clip them off. But if a bunch of leaves are covered in brown spots, you'll need to treat your plant with a fungicide. Try spraying them with a low-level fungicide, such as Captan or Safers brand. Mix the powder with water (according to the product instructions) and spritz it directly onto the leaves. This should take care of your problem.

Problem #4: "Every time I try to repot a plant, it dies."

If you're afraid to move your plant to a new container, you're not alone. Some gardeners (novice and experienced) consider it almost bad luck to replant. But most plants do need new surroundings from time to time. If you allow them to stay "pot bound" for too long, eventually they'll get stressed out, the roots will have nowhere to move, and you'll have to water all the time. Mayhem all around.

There is a trick to safe and effective repotting. First, dump the plant upside down, gently remove it from the pot, and "tease" out the roots a bit, loosening them up. It's okay to repot in the same container—if you want to keep the plant the same size, or you just like the pretty cachepot it fits in. Just make sure there's room in the pot for a half an inch of fresh potting mix all around. If not, you need to upgrade to a bigger size.

Then, pour fresh potting mix into the bottom of the container. Place your plant in the pot, and use a small spade to add more mix around the sides of the pot. Keep turning the pot as you go, and add more of the mixture, patting it down a bit if necessary. The important thing is to be sure that there are no air pockets around the roots. This is the main reason plants have problems with repotting: The roots can die if they're sitting in an air pocket, and you'll wonder, What happened to my poor plant? To avoid these gaps, take a stick or barbecue skewer and poke into the soil all the way around the inside edges of the pot.

Problem #5: "My plant doesn't seem as healthy as it once did, but I haven't changed my routine. What's wrong?"

One way to diagnose the problem is to tip your pot over and play plant doctor. Bring your plant over to a sink and gently tilt it until the soil becomes lose and you can pull the root mass out of the container. Now take a look at the color and condition of the roots. What to watch for:

- **White, plump roots** signify that the plant's in good health and getting enough water.
- **Roots that have brown, rotted ends** in mushy soil indicate that you're overwatering the plant. Perhaps you're still watering your plant at a "summer" rate (when the plant's in high-growth mode), but it's the middle of winter. Time to back off a bit. To revive the plant, snip off the damaged root ends, and replant.
- **Crispy, brittle roots** tell you that the plant's not getting enough water and the potting mix is much too dry. If stepping up your water doesn't help, you may need to repot the plant.

Great Ways to Display

*O*nce you've amassed a few plants that are thriving, you may want to have some fun with their display. Here are a few ideas to help you get the maximum enjoyment out of your new housemates.

Go for group therapy.

One lowly geranium or ribbon fern can look a bit sad sitting all by itself on a table. But a bunch of plants nestled together will give your space a pop of color or turn an overlooked corner into a serene setting. Tray tables or plant stands that use trays are a smart option. You can display several plants at once, while elevating them to window level. Then, if you need to move the plants to the sink or outside, just carry them right on the tray.

Fix your feng shui.

If you have a superstitious side, like me, you may believe that plants can bring good fortune. With feng shui and plants, I figure: It can't hurt, so why not try it? Some green groupings that the Chinese believe to be lucky: Any round-leafed plant—jade, geranium, prayer plant, etc. placed in the southeast corner of your home is supposed to boost your fortune. In fact, jade plants are thought to be so beneficial they're nicknamed "money trees"— good thing they're easy to grow too! To be more successful at work, place any plant in the east, south, or southeast corners of your office. Plants that have dead or dying leaves are thought to bring down the energy level. Makes sense: Who wants to live with a bunch of brown leaves? If you choose the easy growers in this book, your plants will probably look healthy much of the time. But do trim away any old, wilted foliage.

Plant a rock garden.

A smart way to amass your African violets (or any other plant): Place a collection of them on a tray covered in pebbles. Pour water into the tray so the rocks are almost submerged. Then, set the plants on top. This trick helps to keep them moist when the air is dry. It can also be an attractive, Zen-like arrangement.

Set up a window box—indoors.

While window boxes are often used to lend curb appeal to the outside of a home, these versatile planters are perfect for displaying a collection of houseplants on the other side of the pane. Window boxes are available in an array of materials—wood, metal, stone, terracotta—and styles ranging from country to formal. Everyday plants like pothos and heart ivy look much more attractive when they're dressed up in an antique copper planter. Tall, flowering amaryllis seem even more striking when you plant three or four of them in a ceramic or wooden window box. Mix up several houseplants or herbs to create a mini indoor garden. You can use brackets to hang the window boxes indoors, or just place a planter on a sunny sideboard.

Put plastic under wraps.

If your new clivia seems happy in its original nursery pot, but you don't have a ceramic cachepot to set it in, try this idea for sprucing up the container. Take a length of colorful wired ribbon. Glue one end to the top of the pot and wind the ribbon around the plant, circling down to the bottom of the container. This technique will give a boring plastic pot a softer, prettier façade.

Don't forget the bathroom.

It's a natural spot for houseplants because they enjoy the humidity from the shower. If you have a decent-sized bathroom with a Jacuzzi-style tub, place a few ferns or a streptocarpus nearby to create a spa-like environment while you're soaking in the bath.

Foliage
Plants

*Y*ou'll notice that some of the plants in this section (prayer plant, wandering jew, corn plant, jade plant, and others) bloom from time to time. Don't be alarmed! In spite of their occasional, subtle blossoms, these varieties are still considered to be foliage plants because they're cultivated for their leaves.

Arrowhead Plant

(Syngonium podophyllum or *Nephthytis)*

Originally from Mexico and Central America, this super-dependable plant has an unusual habit: Its leaves change shape over time. A young plant seems to have green arrowheads shooting out of its stems. As the syngonium matures, its leaves sprout "wings" or lobes. The more lobes the leaves have, the older the plant. One thing that's consistent about the arrowhead is the attractive foliage that's medium-green, laced with a white veinlike pattern.

BASIC CARE The laidback arrowhead can live almost anywhere. But its ultimate home is a spot that gets bright but filtered light. Try a moderately lit north window or an east-facing window. Check the plant once or twice a week—stick your finger right into the soil—to see if it needs water. You should let it dry out slightly before watering. If the new leaves are looking brown on the edges, you know you're not watering it enough and the air may be too cool or drafty. Likewise, if your arrowhead gets spindly, you're probably watering too much; give it a bit of a rest during the winter months. And if the leaves are very pale, almost colorless, the plant is begging you for fertilizer and may be getting too much sun. Feed it every second or third week during the summer, but cut back to once a month or less during the cold season.

GROW-LIKE-A-PRO TIP Some plants enjoy basking in the sun outdoors during the summer months, but the arrowhead isn't one of them. Because its leaves bleach easily, you're better off keeping your arrowhead in the same place year-round.

Baby's Tears
(Soleirolia soleirolii)

A real softie, this fluffy-looking plant has tons of tiny little leaves. Large, low pots of baby's tears could almost be mistaken for green pillows. I don't recommend napping at the nursery, but feel free to give the plant a pat on the head. There's something about the hundreds of miniature leaves bunched together that beg you to touch them. Now that you've got a sense of this plant's delicate nature, here's the other side of it: A baby's tears is no wimp! In fact, it's deceptively resilient.

BASIC CARE Because it doesn't have dense roots, baby's tears can grow in a shallow bowl. Place your plant in a fairly shady spot; a north window would be fine. If you have an east window that gets just a few hours of sun a day, that will work well too. It does need regular watering, about once or twice a week. Just poke your finger into the potting mix to tell for sure. What makes this creeping variety a cinch to care for? Like a real baby, it lets you know when it wants something. Are the leaves flattened out and looking droopy? Baby needs a drink. Tending to this plant will be even more of a no-brainer if you set the pot on a saucer to help keep the humidity up. But don't let it sit in a puddle; empty any excess after you've finished watering.

GROW-LIKE-A-PRO TIP Baby's tears spreads quickly and can start to get bushy. Cut it back every six months or so and more tiny leaves will grow in, renewing the plant's fresh, dense foliage.

Cast-Iron Plant
(*Aspidistra elatior*)

From the name alone, you know that this one isn't about to go down without a fight. Not surprisingly, it's also dubbed the barroom plant. The wide, dark, straplike leaves grow at a snail's pace. The cast iron can survive in low-light conditions, which made it particularly popular in Victorian times when homes were dimly lit by gaslight. Because of its "slow down, you move too fast" attitude, the cast iron also doesn't require much water.

BASIC CARE The cast iron is truly a friend to the forgetful plant owner, as it can get by in a variety of conditions. Ideally, you should place it in bright, indirect light (a spot near a north or east window would suffice) and check it about once a week for watering. Push your finger into the soil; if you find that it's dry several inches down, it's time to give the plant a drink. Missed a week here or there? No problem. This sturdy specimen rarely shows the signs of neglect. Should you seriously overwater the cast iron, you'll notice that the ends of the leaves will start to yellow. Hold back and the cast iron will snap into shape again. If you feed it with an all-purpose fertilizer in the spring, you may see some star-shaped flowers right along the soil line.

GROW-LIKE-A-PRO TIP If you're ever repotting the cast iron—and you won't need to do this very often—you can split it into two and multiply your collection of carefree greenery (See "Grow Forth and Multiply" on page 17 for tips on how best to go about this).

Century Plant

(*Agave americana*)

Originally from Mexico, this cousin of the aloe plant has spiny-tipped green leaves with thin yellow or white stripes along its edges. The leaves grow in a rosette shape and can reach several feet in length. Be careful not to prick yourself or touch the plant's juices. Unlike the soothing aloe, the sap of the century plant can give you an itchy rash; handle it gingerly. As long as it gets plenty of light, the century plant can be left alone for weeks at a time.

BASIC CARE Being a desert dweller, a century plant prefers direct sun and warm temperatures. A south-facing window would be best, but it can certainly survive in less light. The century is also related to the cactus, so it needs very little watering—about once every three weeks to once a month. It takes ages for the "century" to bloom, if it does at all, hence its name. But in reality, it will flower about every ten or twenty years, not every hundred. Just don't hold your breath! Fertilize this plant about four times a year.

GROW-LIKE-A-PRO TIP You only need to repot the century plant about once every four or five years. But when you do transplant, fill the container with a potting mix that's graded for cactus.

Chinese Evergreen
(Aaglaonema commutatum)

Is your apartment seriously lacking in sunny windows? Want some greenery in a room on the shady side of your house? Consider a low-light-loving Chinese evergreen. You'll see this tropical and its close cousin, the pewter plant, all over the place—in malls, in hotel lobbies, in dimly lit restaurants. And if it can survive there, your home will seem like plant nirvana. If you're lucky, your Chinese evergreen will occasionally bloom, with pale-green flowers, followed by berries.

BASIC CARE Another slow grower, this is a blasé beauty that you can forget to water and not feel an ounce of guilt. Placed anywhere near (but not necessarily in) a north or east window, the aglaonema is destined to live happily ever after. During the winter months, you only need to water it once a week or even every other week. Water more frequently from spring to autumn (a couple of times a week or as often as you notice the soil feels dry to the touch, using the finger test). Fertilize lightly: once in spring and once again in midsummer, using a diluted liquid fertilizer. The Chinese evergreen doesn't need a new home as often as some plants; repot it just once every three years.

GROW-LIKE-A-PRO TIP To promote full, lush foliage, mist the plant regularly—it likes moist air.

Corn Plant
(Dracaena fragrans massangeana)

True to its name, this variety can grow to mimic a tall, leafy corn stalk. It has broad, dark green leaves (some may be striped with a bit of yellow) that arch out from the woody center. You need to give your corn plenty of open space. Over time, this narrow plant can reach as high as your ceiling, if you let it. Fortunately, the ultimate height is up to you. Too tall for your taste? The rough-and-tumble corn plant doesn't mind being beheaded from time to time. Just chop off the top six inches or so and it keeps right on growing.

BASIC CARE The corn plant tolerates a wide range of temperatures and prefers moderate, indirect light; an east window would be fine. This plant likes a break from the sun in the afternoon. Though very versatile, if this dracaena gets too much sun, the leaves will start to develop brown spots. Keep the soil lightly moist—but not soggy! Occasional watering—once a week or so—is fine. A mature corn plant may bloom and its fluffy pink or purplish flowers (they look like clover or oddly colored dandelions) give off a powerful, sweet fragrance. Fertilize your corn plant a couple of times during the summer; it doesn't need any food during the colder months.

GROW-LIKE-A-PRO TIP Over time, the woodlike canes of the corn plant can get top-heavy, which could cause it to tip over. Be sure to stake or secure the canes to keep them stable and healthy.

41

Dumb Cane

(Dieffenbachia amoena Tropic Snow or *Dieffenbachia hilo)*

Perhaps this lush tropical plant is simply compensating for its IQ. All it needs are a moderately bright window, a little water, and it yields huge leaves that may be speckled with pretty, cream-colored patterns. Actually, the plant's name was coined because of its poisonous sap; even a small amount in the mouth (don't try this at home) would cause your tongue to swell, rendering you "dumb." But since you're not planning to drink the plant's juice, you can simply enjoy the lush, low-maintenance foliage. If you have pets, you should put your dumb cane on a shelf or in a room where your dog or cat won't be able reach it.

BASIC CARE The indirect light of an east-facing window will suit the dumb cane. If the leaves appear yellow and curled, they're getting a sunburn; move it to a spot that isn't as bright. Check your dieffenbachia about once or twice a week during the active growing months (April to October) to see if it's dry and wanting water. During the summer months, feed it about once a month with a diluted liquid fertilizer. Over the cold season, you can leave your dumb cane with less water and it will continue to thrive.

GROW-LIKE-A-PRO TIP About the only way to do this plant in is to drown it. If you're too zealous with the watering can, you could wind up rotting this plant's roots. So go easy. Neglect is best!

Dwarf Schefflera
(Schefflera arbicola)

If you love the look of glossy, shiny leaves, bring home a schefflera. Whether you pick a dwarf variety (which has smaller leaves and is also called the Dwarf umbrella tree) or a standard schefflera, you'll get a sizeable, accommodating plant that makes a statement in any room. Some have leaves dappled with yellow designs.

BASIC CARE Scheffleras like morning light and cooler temperatures. But they tolerate anything from an eastern to western exposure, and a north window would be suitable during the summer. The plant is forgiving to say the least. My dwarf version has been thriving in an east window that's mostly blocked by a pine tree. If it doesn't get enough light, the plant may thin out a bit, but it won't die. Keep it evenly moist, checking the soil about once a week; fertilize monthly throughout the year. If it isn't pruned from time to time, it can reach heights of greater than six feet.

GROW-LIKE-A-PRO TIP Dust the leaves occasionally, or mist them with water, to remove any dirt and bring out the shine.

English Ivy
(Hedera helix)

This pretty plant has medium-green leaves tinged with ivory edges. You can coax an English ivy into a topiary because it likes to twist and climb. Or try setting your ivy in a hanging basket.

BASIC CARE The agreeable English ivy likes its light but prefers somewhat cooler temperatures—less than 70 degrees during the day and 40 to 50 at night. Like the hoards of Britons who head to the Algarve and Greece every winter, this particular ivy enjoys its sun. Find it a well-lit perch. But, just like many Brits, this ivy is also prone to sunburn; shield it from bright afternoon light during the summer months. The ivy doesn't need lots of water; let it dry out between watering. Once the soil feels dry, you can give it a decent drink—let the water run out of the bottom of the pot and onto a saucer. But then drain the excess water in the saucer; don't let the ivy rest in water. This plant favors a bit of humidity, so give it a misting every so often. To keep it looking lush, use a diluted liquid fertilizer every other week during the warmer months.

GROW-LIKE-A-PRO TIP Like all ivies, this one could be susceptible to mites. If you really want to avoid pests, bring your English ivy to the sink once a week. Give the leaves a shower, using the hose attachment. Yes, this step takes extra time but could pay off in the long run.

Fatsia

(Fatsia japonica)

Native to Japan, this handsome plant has lovely, glossy green leaves that look almost like those from a maple tree. Fatsia, also called Japanese aralia, is actually a tropical evergreen that can eventually grow to more than five feet tall. Great for offices, it will hang in there even if it's only exposed to artificial light. Once in a while, you may see white flowers and berries.

BASIC CARE Your fatsia will be happy any place that gets a medium amount of light: an east or west window would be ideal. Keep the soil reasonably moist; check once a week to see if the potting mix feels dry. During the warmer months, fatsia enjoys extra water. But in the winter, you should let it dry out a bit before adding water. If the leaves turn yellow, that means the conditions are too warm and dry. It prefers a cooler locale. Feed your fatsia about once a month from spring through the summer. If your plant is outgrowing your space, cut it back in the spring.

GROW-LIKE-A-PRO TIP If you want to add more fatsia to your collection, this plant can easily reproduce from stem cuttings.

49

Heart Ivy
(Philodendron scandens oxycardium)

Sometimes labeled heart-leaf philodendron, this vinelike plant with glossy, heart-shaped leaves spreads like wildfire. An idiot-proof favorite, it can handle all kinds of abuse. So your motto should be "Absence makes the heart (ivy) grow faster."

BASIC CARE Heart ivy doesn't need tons of light, nor tons of water. Place it just about anywhere: a north window, an east or west window, or no window, and it will grow like a champ. Because of its low light requirements, heart ivy is a smart choice for an office or any room that has limited light. Though this plant doesn't mind low humidity that's common in most homes, you should keep the soil moist. Just check it about once a week or so to see if it's in need of a drink. For lush foliage, fertilize your heart ivy about once a month.

GROW-LIKE-A-PRO TIP If you notice the leaves are turning yellow on your philodendron (a rare occurrence), you're probably watering it too much. Ease up, and your plant will get green again. Another remedy for yellowing leaves: Try giving the plant just a bit more light.

Jade Plant
(*Crassula ovata* or *Crassula argentea*)

Originally from South Africa, this Zen plant has smooth, round leaves that symbolize vitality. Practitioners of feng shui believe that this miniature tree is a lucky plant. If you place it in a south-east-corner window, so the wisdom goes, you'll increase your wealth. Its thick, rubbery leaves can get so heavy that the plant tips to one side. To prevent the lopsided look, snip off the excess as needed. Because it's a succulent, the jade doesn't need much water; it can store water and nutrients inside.

BASIC CARE Jade likes a fairly bright windowsill—west or south would be ideal—but the plant happily tolerates less light if necessary. During the summer, water about once a week, and fertilize every other week with African violet food. It needs very little watering during the cooler months; water about once every six to eight weeks in winter. Remember to use tepid, not cold, water; chilly water can stress out the otherwise agreeable jade. By giving the jade a period of rest (i.e., little water, no fertilizer), you may be treated to little white or pink blossoms. As for containers, the jade plant doesn't need a new home very often. Repot it only if you see roots poking out from the bottom.

GROW-LIKE-A-PRO TIP The graceful jade plant has a taste for fresh air. So, open the windows in the warmer months (just avoid any cold drafts). Think about placing it outside during the summer, giving it some protection from the hot afternoon sun.

Janet Craig
(Dracaena deremensis 'Janet Craig')

Named for a nurseryman's wife, Janet Craig has broad, long, dark-green leaves that flow out gracefully from its stalk. What makes this variety such a no-brainer? It can grow in low light and it doesn't mind dry conditions. If you're interested in purifying the air in your home or office, Janet Craig and other dracaenas are a wise choice; this plant was noted in the NASA Clean Air Study to be helpful for removing formaldehyde from the air. This particular dracaena could be mistaken for a palm, but it's actually most closely related to the lily family. Its sister, the striped dracaena, is also a cinch to grow.

BASIC CARE Janet Craig thrives in a warmer climate: about 75 degrees is perfect, but she'll fare alright in cooler temps too. She doesn't like too much sun; the indirect light of a north or east window would be perfect. As for watering, check the soil at least once a week. If the soil is slightly dry to the touch, it's time to water your dracaena. Just be sure to let the soil dry out before watering her again. If you overexpose Janet Craig to the sun, her leaves will start to yellow. Just prune off the unhealthy leaves and give her some shade. You won't have to do much fertilizing here. You can skip it in the winter completely and just fertilize once a month in the spring and summer to encourage growth.

GROW-LIKE-A-PRO TIP Swipe this plant's shiny leaves with a damp cloth every now and then. This will get rid of dust and keep her looking lovely.

Lacy-Tree Philodendron
(Philodendron bipinnatifidum or *philodendron selloum)*

Another member of that überhardy family, the philodendrons, the lacy-tree variety has shiny leaves with "fingers" on each side. This beautiful, bushy plant grows out and around. A mature lacy-tree can stretch out to nearly five feet around, so you need to give it plenty of space to spread out; a large corner of a room should be fine.

BASIC CARE This philodendron prefers moderately bright light; an east- or west-facing window would be fine. If you have a sunnier spot, it won't mind the extra light. Let the lacy-tree dry out between waterings (use the finger test). Feed your philodendron about once a month; just a few drops of the liquid fertilizer will suit it just fine. Like the Janet Craig dracaena, this plant is good for your health: Its large leaves remove certain pollutants, such as formaldehyde, from the air.

GROW-LIKE-A-PRO TIP If you don't have the space for a lacy-tree, there's a smaller variety available called Xanadu. The Xanadu also has downsized leaves and will mature to a size of about three feet wide.

LADY PALM
(Rhapis excelsa)

One of the most versatile, easygoing palms, this native of southern China has sturdy canes that shoot out broad, shiny, bright-green leaves. In a greenhouse, the rhapis excelsa grows rapidly (eight to twelve inches a year) and it can reach a giant height of fourteen feet tall! But under home conditions, it's much more manageable. Rhapis excelsa is a fairly expensive plant, but fans say that the cost is worth it because she's so simple to care for. This is one adaptable lady—she can live in cold or hot temperatures. And dry air doesn't bother her a bit. She'll adjust to almost any living conditions.

BASIC CARE Allow this slow-growing palm to dry out a bit between waterings. Set your lady friend in bright, indirect light (an east-facing window would work). If the lady palm gets too much sun, her leaves will start to turn to a bleached-out, yellowy look. If you notice the leaves are fading, move her to a shadier spot. Your pretty palm won't need much fertilizer, but do plant it in a rich mixture, like an African violet potting mix.

GROW-LIKE-A-PRO TIP If you repot a lady palm in the spring or summer, while it's actively growing, you can divide it and cultivate sister plants.

Medicine Plant or Aloe Vera
(Aloe barbadensis)

There are dozens of hybrids of durable, succulent aloe. But this particular spiky-leafed species has been harvested and prized for its healing properties for centuries. Break off a leaf, squeeze out the sap, and the gel really helps to soothe the sting of sunburn, to treat cuts, and to ease other skin conditions. The plump leaves grow out from the center of the plant and can reach two feet in length. If you keep it outside during the warmer months, your aloe plant may occasionally bloom into tubular yellow flowers.

BASIC CARE Place the slow-growing aloe plant near a window where it will get plenty of bright light: West or south are fine but it can adjust to an eastern exposure too. You may want to keep your aloe near the kitchen for easy access; in case of cooking mishaps, you've got an instant burn remedy on hand. Aloe really is simple to grow. During the winter, it only needs water about once or twice a month. When the weather warms up, bring your plant outside for the summer, and check it from time to time to make sure that the soil doesn't dry out completely in the hot sun. Over the summer, feed your aloe plant about once a month. It doesn't need fertilizer during the cold season.

GROW-LIKE-A-PRO TIP Going away on an extended trip? You can help your aloe plant to survive for more than a month by simply covering it loosely with plastic wrap or a clear plastic bag. This helps to create a more humid environment, keeping it moist until you return. If you want to protect a group of plants while you're on vacation, place them in a sink lined with wet newspapers and cover with plastic wrap.

Parlor Palm
(Chamaedorea elegans)

A graceful palm that can grow to be six feet tall, the parlor has large, featherlike fronds. The common name comes from the fact that these classic plants were a staple in the parlors of Victorian homes. The elegant parlor tolerates low light, so it's one of the easiest palms to grow indoors. On mature plants, you may notice some berrylike flowers from time to time.

BASIC CARE When you think of palms, what comes to mind? Swaying trees in a tropical locale? A hammock and frozen margaritas? Well, indoor palms like it hot too—or at least warm. Cozy temperatures and balmy breezes are best for the parlor palm. Settle them away from cold, drafty windows or rooms that you don't keep well heated in the winter months. This plant will thrive in an east- or north-facing window; somewhat limited sunlight won't hurt it a bit. Try to keep the soil slightly moist at all times. Check it regularly and water as needed. But hold back a bit in the winter: It needs less H_2O during the colder months. But it will benefit from fertilizing once a month in winter, and every other week during the summer.

GROW-LIKE-A-PRO TIP Mist your parlor palm every so often to help boost the humidity. If you're going to repot your parlor palm, blend a bit of sand into an African violet potting mix.

Ponytail Palm
(Beaucarnea recurvata)

A native of Mexico, this plant is sometimes called the bottle palm. The long, slender leaves burst out of a knot, hence the name "ponytail." The plant defies its drama-queen guise by being decidedly low maintenance: It grows slowly and needs very little water in the winter months.

BASIC CARE The ponytail palm likes its sun—try a western or southern exposure. But being such an agreeable specimen, it can also get by with less light, if necessary. Since this plant comes from a desert climate, it has no trouble adjusting to a warm, dry environment (the conditions in most people's homes in the middle of winter). The swollen "knot" on this plant's trunk is actually a reservoir for storing water. So you can forget about watering this one for a month at a time, and it won't look worse for the wear.

GROW-LIKE-A-PRO TIP Don't worry if a few of the leaves have brown tips. If they're bothering you, just cut off the leaf and a new one will grow in. To avoid brown tipping, keep the ponytail evenly moist. When the conditions change too dramatically—the plant goes from superdry to drenched—the tips start to show it.

Pothos
(Epipremnum aureum)

You've heard that diamonds are forever. Well, if you're lusting for something shiny and long-lasting, save some money and invest in a pothos instead. Also known as devil's ivy, this vinelike plant with glossy, heart-shaped leaves is almost oblivious to abuse. Ignore it. Neglect it. And this cheerful plant will keep right on growing. Beware: It spreads quickly. You practically can't stop it from expan-ding, and you'll probably have to cut it back regularly to keep it from taking over your living room. With just minimal watering, this forgiving species will sprout seemingly endless cascades of green leaves tinged with white or yellow. For a touch of dramatic color, consider the new neon pothos. It's just as easy to grow as the classic pothos, but its leaves are a bold chartreuse green.

BASIC CARE Stick a pothos almost anywhere—on your desk, on top of the TV, in a random corner. Yes, it likes a little sunlight now and then, but the artificial rays of your lamps are often enough to keep it going. Water only about once a week or less during the cold months. If your pothos's vines start creeping out of control, give it a trim now and then. With this plant, it's okay to play with the scissors and snip off some of the trailing stems and leaves on a regular basis. Of course, new ones will grow back in their place, but you can enjoy the groomed look in the meantime.

GROW-LIKE-A-PRO TIP Few people have difficulty with this hyperhardy plant. But if you happen to notice the leaves black-ening on the ends, you're simply trying too hard—overwatering or giving it too much fertilizer. This is one plant that seems to prefer being left alone. So, snip off the damaged leaves and let the pothos do its thing.

Prayer Plant
(Maranta leuconeura)

The large, lovely leaves on this calming plant are green with a dark spotted pattern and pinkish veins. What's most unusual about this accommodating variety is the way it got its name: At night (or in darkness), the leaves fold up, just like hands praying.

BASIC CARE The prayer plant prefers bright but indirect light. But it can get by on less. Try an east or west window. Prayer plants take a break during the chilly winter months, so they need less water. Wait until the soil feels dry to the touch to water. During the active growing season, keep the prayer plant evenly moist. It's important for it to have good drainage (don't let it sit in a saucer of water). In the spring and summer, watch for the prayer plant to shoot up tiny white flowers. During the summer, feed every two weeks with a basic fertilizer.

GROW-LIKE-A-PRO TIP In the colder months, prayer plants may react to the dry air, with some of its leaves turning brown along the edges. To correct the problem, group it with a bunch of plants to keep up the humidity. Or just set a bowl of water nearby.

Rosemary
(*Rosmarinus officinalis*)

A plant with a refreshing pine scent, rosemary is a member of the evergreen family. If you're a cook, you'll love having this fragrant, flavorful herb in fresh supply in your kitchen—just pluck off a few needles, chop, and add to chicken, lamb, and many other dishes. And it's super easy to grow. I've had great luck with a rosemary plant I picked up at a local plant sale. What started as just a couple of inches of green has taken over a large ceramic cachepot in a matter of months. The rosemary spread quickly during the summer months on a warm, partial sun windowsill on my back porch; it didn't miss a beat when I left it outside as the fall temps turned quite cool; and during the winter, it's faring well on a cool, northwest-facing window. How's that for flexible?

BASIC CARE House your rosemary plant where it will get at least four hours of sun during the warmer months, when you should fertilize it about every two weeks. It will survive on less sun in the winter and only needs fertilizer about once a month. One of the reasons rosemary is so simple to care for: It doesn't need much water. You can just check the soil about once a week. If you poke your finger into the soil and it feels dry, it's time to water.

GROW-LIKE-A-PRO TIP It's a good idea to repot your rosemary plant once a year. If you notice that you're having to water it more frequently than normal, it may need a larger pot. But you can also train it to stay in the same container: Just snip the roots about an inch and trim off some clusters of rosemary needles. Bon appetit.

Rubber Tree
(*Ficus elastica*)

If weeks went by and you forgot you even owned a rubber plant, chances are it would still be faithfully growing along. I've had a rubber plant sitting in the corner of my office for almost six years now. At one point, the plant had only occasional fluorescent light to keep it growing. And I confess that months at a time went by when I never even looked at it, much less watered it. And it's still alive! Only when I happen to catch a glimpse of the thing out of the corner of my eye do I water it. Not that I recommend this type of care, of course. But, as you might expect, the rubber plant always bounces back.

BASIC CARE Place your rubber plant near a medium-light window. It needs some sun, but not a lot. You should water it about once or twice a week; give the soil a good soak, but be sure to let it dry out between waterings. Give the rubber plant even less H_2O in the winter when it won't do much growing; once every other week or even every month should do the trick.

GROW-LIKE-A-PRO TIP Don't be concerned if some of the lower leaves drop off. As the top leaves start to grow, this will happen naturally. The rubber tree can happily live in the same pot, same soil for three years at a time. When you do repot, you may want to try potting mix that's designed for cactus—it drains well, which is something the rubber plant needs.

Screw Pine

(Pandanus veitchii or *Pandanus utilis)*

You can bring a taste of the South Pacific into your home with this handsome, hard-to-kill plant. Notice how the long, swordlike leaves twist into a spiral pattern, and you'll know where this prickly specimen got its name. The term "screw" is apt for other reasons too: Quite simply, the plant is tough as nails. While a pandanus looks like a palm and it's called a pine, in fact, it doesn't qualify as either. The term "pine" came about because in its native tropical habitat the plant produces a fruit that looks like a pineapple.

BASIC CARE The screw pine does enjoy the light; several hours of direct sun each day (east or west window) would be optimal. But if you place this plant in a shadier spot, it won't miss a beat. Make enough room for this palmlike plant. It can grow up to four feet, resembling a mini tree. As long as you give it some shade, the screw pine enjoys being outdoors during the summer months. Like so many of our easy-care plants, the screw pine needs more water in the warm season and less during the winter. After watering, check it about a week or more later. Stick your finger into the soil; the potting mix should be quite dry (about two inches down) before you water again.

GROW-LIKE-A-PRO TIP If you want to add to your Hawaiian houseplant collection, watch for the suckers—baby plants that grow up from the roots—to poke up from the soil. You can pull up a few suckers, and if they have enough roots of their own, pot them to create new screw pines.

Southern Yew

(Podocarpus macrophyllus maki)

Also known as the Buddhist pine or the Japanese yew, this slow-growing, stately evergreen with dark, needle-like leaves can grow to be a sizable four to five feet tall. But it's easy to keep it to that height or shorter through regular pruning. Because it's simple to prune, this plant is often shaped into topiaries. You'll also spot this bushy, tree-type plant in offices, shopping malls, and airports.

BASIC CARE One of the ultimate owner-friendly plants, the southern yew can handle anything from full sunshine to mostly shade. But its ideal location is in a spot where it receives bright, indirect light, such an east or west window. Feel free to have a senior moment when it comes to watering this sturdy pine. During the winter season, the southern yew only needs an occasional drink, about once every couple of weeks. Check the soil a bit more regularly in the warmer months. This semitropical tree can thrive in a range of temperatures. You only need to feed the houseplant twice a year—once in spring and once in summer with a mild fertilizer.

GROW-LIKE-A-PRO TIP In spite of the fact that it's called the *southern* yew, this plant actually enjoys chillier temperatures. If you keep it in a room that gets cool at night or near a drafty window, it won't mind a bit.

Snake Plant
(*Sansevieria trifasciata*)

I have to go out on a limb and declare this the number-one most indestructible houseplant of all time. In the strongest plant competition, the snake is poised to bring home the trophy. You can water it (or not), give it sun (or shade), and the tall, spiky leaves will continue to stand tall—no matter what the conditions. Want to take long vacations and never have to hire a plant-sitter? The snake plant's your best bet. For the same reason, the snake (also called the mother-in-law's tongue) is a perfect choice for offices where there's little light and your attention is always on other things.

BASIC CARE You can put this plant just about anywhere—across the room from a window, under mostly artificial light, and it won't mind a bit. Water it when it occurs to you. You can often go for weeks at a time without watering, particularly during the winter months. Fertilize the snake plant once a month from spring through fall.

GROW-LIKE-A-PRO TIP What makes this plant attractive are its lofty, shiny leaves. Dust the leaves from time to time and wipe with a damp cloth to keep them looking glossy.

Spider Plant
(Chlorophytum comosum)

So popular it could be called the people's plant, this carefree,
cascading variety works particularly well in hanging containers. Its
leaves are long and thin, striped with yellow or cream. What's fun
about the spider plant are its babies—it shoots off little "mini
spiders" that trail down around the edges. If you clip off these
offspring and set them in water, they'll sprout roots, and you can
turn them into new plants.

BASIC CARE In order for the spider to produce "spiderlets," it
needs enough light. A bright north window would work fine, as
would a spot where it will get morning or afternoon sun. Full-day
sun is too much for the spider, so avoid overly sunny exposures.
Water about twice a week or less during the winter; poke your
finger in the soil to check).

This plant's thick roots tend to fill a pot quickly, so you may
want to repot once a year in the spring. If the leaves get brown on
the ends, don't fret. This is common with spider plants; just snip
off the dead part and move on.

GROW-LIKE-A-PRO TIP Generally a cinch to care for, the spider
plant has one occasional glitch: It seems to be more prone to little
bugs than some other plants. See some mites? Don't panic. See p.
20 for easy ways to get rid of them. To keep the pests from
returning, consider watering less frequently. Little gnats breed in
moist soil; if you let the potting mix dry out between watering,
you can shut out the bugs. Remember, a laissez-faire approach
works wonders with low-maintenance plants like the spider.

Table Fern
(*Pteris*)

Does the word "fern" strike fear in your novice gardener's heart? Don't let it. For sure, many ferns are difficult to grow, but some beautiful exceptions to the rule are any of the *Pteris* family, which includes the "table" fern, the "brake" fern, and the "ribbon" fern. Though they have frilly, lacy-edged leaves, these ferns defy their delicate nature. They're surprisingly robust and less fussy than their cousins. Note: Another easy-care fern to try that's not part of the *Pteris* clan is the Dallas fern.

BASIC CARE Either an east- or north-facing window with just partial sunlight makes a fine home for the low-light-loving table fern. The *Pteris* family of ferns needs less water than most. It's okay to let the soil dry out a bit between watering. As with so many other plants in this book, check the soil once a week to see if it feels moist or dry and water accordingly. These ferns do like their humidity, however, so give them a quick misting from time to time. Or group a collection of ferns together; they'll stay moist for longer that way.

GROW-LIKE-A-PRO TIP Are the leaves turning yellow and wilting? That's a sure sign that you're watering too much. Back off and your fern will bounce back.

Wandering Jew
(*Tradescantia zebrina* or *Zebrina pendula*)

Also known as the wandering sailor, this fast-growing, vine-like plant has cascading stems that are covered in small leaves striped with white or purple. This plant will look lush throughout the warmer months, when it likes to be moved outside, and will bloom with petite lavender-colored flowers. In the late winter months, it may start to look a bit punky—but don't try to give it a makeover—the handsome houseplant will come back in full force once the spring arrives.

BASIC CARE The wandering jew enjoys medium to full sunlight. It needs regular watering—about twice a week from April to October and very little water during the cold season. If your plant appears spindly or the leaves start to look "crisp," spritz it with a spray bottle to boost humidity. To coax new growth in the center of the plant, pinch or trim back the stems. In the cold season, the inner vines and leaves may start to turn brown—they're not getting enough light because they're hiding underneath other foliage. Don't worry about it. Just grab a bunch of the withering stems and yank on them, pulling them right off the plant. Don't be afraid to give this plant a trim; its vines will grow back in no time.

GROW-LIKE-A-PRO TIP If your wandering jew is blooming, enjoy the flowers but snip them off as soon as they start to fade. The dead flowers can drain energy from the plant.

Flowering
Plants

*W*ith these plants, it's all about the blossoms. If you're a flower lover, the list that follows includes some of the easiest plants to keep blooming—and to keep alive!

African Violet
(*Saintpaulia*)

A queen among houseplants, the African violet can bloom into delicate violet, blue, pink, and white flowers at almost any time during the year. It has dark-green, rounded leaves that have a bit of fuzz on them.

BASIC CARE An east-facing window is ideal for the African violet for most of the year; during the winter months, a southern exposure would work well too. All plants should get room-temperature water, but this one can even benefit from slightly lukewarm water. If you use H_2O that's too cold, it will cause spots on the African violet's leaves. Feed this plant weekly with a liquid fertilizer. The biggest concern people have with African violets is that they're not flowering enough (or at all). The reason is simple: It's not getting enough light. Check the sunlight and move your African violet to a sunnier spot. If you do this and continue to fertilize, those pretty blooms will be on the way.

GROW-LIKE-A-PRO TIP Occasionally, the queen gets too many "crowns" (clusters of leaves at the base), and you need to snip them off to encourage healthy growth and flowers.

Amaryllis
(Hippeastrum hortorum)

An amaryllis plant is truly your ticket to looking like a plant genius without really trying. These seasonal showstoppers take just six to eight weeks to bloom. I stuck my first potted bulb in a kitchen windowsill, watering it maybe once a week. A few weeks later, the plant's bud opened up into three huge scarlet blossoms. The traditional color is red, but there are many varieties from nymph, a white flower with stripes of pink, to Solomon, a salmon-colored bloom.

BASIC CARE It's a cinch to grow an amaryllis from a bulb that's already planted in soil and sprouting a bit of green. Check the stalks. If you see two or three (instead of just one), buy it—you've got a bulb that will produce twice or triple the number of flowers. It's also quite simple, and cheaper, to plant your own bulbs. This flower will even grow in a pile of pebbles—that's how determined it is to bloom. Know that the amaryllis isn't a year-round plant. Once the flowers have faded, take the bulb in its pot and set it in a cool, dark place (a basement perhaps) and allow it to be dormant. You can repot the bulb next fall, but if you're fortunate enough to get a second round of blooms, they won't be nearly as big and bold as the first. So if you love amaryllis flowers, you're better off buying a few new bulbs next season.

GROW-LIKE-A-PRO TIP If you live in the Deep South, you can plant amaryllis in the garden. These bulbs will produce a wonderful display next year, and for years to come. In sunnier zones, the light conditions are just right for reblooming.

Clivia
(Clivia miniata)

Sometimes known as the flame lily or kaffir lily, the clivia has thick, dark-green, strappy leaves like a cast-iron plant, but it also blooms into beautiful, abundant orange flowers once a year. The sunburst of blossoms grows in a cluster on a stem, typically appearing in March or April. For a flowering plant, the clivia is seriously low-maintenance. Don't have much light? Don't sweat it. Want to take a two-week vacation and forget about your clivia? Ditto.

BASIC CARE Clivia enjoy an eastern exposure, but they can easily grow in less light. In fact, even a dimly lit corner of your living room will do. For most of the year, you'll want to water your clivia using the standard "finger" test: If the soil's dry an inch down, it's time to grab the watering can. You should feed your clivia frequently during the summer months. But the trick to ensuring gorgeous blooms is to let the plant dry out a bit during the months of October, November, and December. This will actually encourage the clivia to blossom in the new year. So, while you're in the middle of the busy holiday season, take a break on watering. Only water when the soil is dry two inches down. Then, resume your regular watering schedule in January. By the end of the month, you should start to see spikes growing up in the center of the plant. And in February (or March), you'll be rewarded with those vibrant orange flowers.

GROW-LIKE-A-PRO TIP Clivia is one of those varieties that likes to stay put. Keep it in the same pot for five years or more and you'll have a happy plant.

Dancing Ladies
(*Streptocarpella*)

If you want year-round color in a plant that's a cinch to maintain, consider this blooming beauty. With its velvety leaves and abundant lavender or purple blooms, dancing ladies adds a touch of softness to a room. The violetesque flowers shoot up on ultrathin stems, so they appear to be floating (or dancing) above the leaves. Treat this plant, and all members of the *Streptocarpus* family, as you would its close cousin, the African violet.

BASIC CARE To coax your dancing ladies into constant bloom, indulge it in plenty of sunshine. This plant loves light; it could grow in an east, west or northwest window. But shelter it from the harsh southern sun during the summer months, otherwise its delicate leaves could be scorched. Dancing ladies doesn't mind drying out a bit before you water it. As usual, do the finger check and water as needed. Fertilize your streptocarpella with a weak liquid solution every time you water to promote plentiful flowers. This is one plant that likes to be picked on, meaning, pinch off dead leaves and wilted blooms on a regular basis. I'm always picking at mine, plucking off a brown stem here, deadheading a flower there, and it blooms month after month. A little plant "grooming" can relieve stress—and it beats biting your nails!

GROW-LIKE-A-PRO TIP If you want to give your dancing ladies a boost during the warm season, fertilize with fish emulsion. Also try Schultz African violet food (in liquid form). Don't expose the plant to cold rainwater; and, of course, water with only room-temperature or warmer H_2O. Cold liquid will cause black spots on the suedelike leaves.

Geranium
(*Pelargonium hortorum*)

You can't avoid running into this plant during the summer months—it's sold everywhere from the supermarket to your local nursery. The geranium has rounded, ruffled leaves and will give you plentiful, colorful blooms during the warmer months. There are many varieties, with flower shades of white, pink, red, salmon, and even purple. Geraniums are considered to be a symbol of friendship. Try placing a pair of pots by your front door—a welcome sign for guests—or group a collection of the scented variety on your deck, a fresh backdrop for outdoor meals. Then, you can bring the plants indoors for winter, and they'll continue to grow and bloom once again in the spring.

BASIC CARE Geraniums are sun lovers. Stick them on a porch or in a west- or south-facing window, and they'll thrive. The soil needs to dry out between waterings. Check it several times a week during the summer months; it can get dry quickly. If you keep the potting mix too moist, the geranium could be prone to a fungal disease, which causes black spots on the leaves. To encourage new blooms, deadhead the old flowers (pinch them off), just as they're starting to fade.

GROW-LIKE-A-PRO TIP If your geranium has lots of thick foliage but no flowers, the soil may be too rich. To remedy the problem,you can practice something called traumatic stimulation. Sounds unsettling, but all it really means is cutting back the roots. Take your plant out of its pot, trim the roots back a bit, and repot. This simple technique will encourage more flower buds for the next growing cycle.

Kalanchoe
(Kalanchoe blossfeldiana)

A pretty plant with glossy, dark, ridged leaves, the kalanchoe shoots up buds with tiny clusters of yellow, pink, red, and other vibrant colored flowers. Some people treat kalanchoe, also called the flaming Katy, as a one-time bloomer: When the flowers are gone, they toss the plant. But the kalanchoe will flower again (twice every year) if you care for it properly—though the flowers aren't quite as bold the second time around. While you're waiting for it to bloom again, the foliage is quite attractive.

BASIC CARE The kalanchoe likes bright, indirect light in the summer months. In winter, you could move it to a spot with even more sun, such as a south or southeast window. But it will live with less. This is a perfect plant to keep in a guest room or any room you don't use very often. Why? If you want to encourage it to flower again, you need to limit the amount of light it gets to ten hours a day. Watch for flowers in the spring, and then again in the fall. Be sure to let the soil dry out between waterings. The plant needs very little water during the cooler months. The more you water, the bigger the leaves will get. Feed your kalanchoe every couple of weeks, from May to September, using a diluted liquid fertilizer. Pinch off the stalks when the flowers start to fade.

GROW-LIKE-A-PRO TIP Cut your kalanchoe back after it blooms. If the plant has fewer stems, this will lead to more flowers in the future.

Peace Lily
(*Spathiphyllum*)

This beautiful flowering plant with dark, graceful leaves gives new meaning to the word "hardy." It requires more watering than some, but it lets you know right away when it needs attention—the leaves start to droop, as if crying out, "Water me, water me!" As long as you keep this one in a spot you check regularly and "listen" to your lily, it will guide you to what's needed.

BASIC CARE Place it in indirect sunlight and obey the peace lily's demands when it tells you it's parched (i.e., water when you notice it's looking limp). One reason for this plant's popularity is that, in addition to being easy to grow, it also sends up shoots throughout the year that bloom into delicate white, spadelike flowers. To encourage your peace lily to sprout more lilies you should fertilize the plant once every other week, beginning in spring. Once the flowers die (they will discolor or turn green), remove them or the dying blooms will take energy from the plant. Don't just snip off the heads of the flowers. Cut them off at the stem (just above the node) and get rid of that as well. Another benefit to the peace lily: fresher air! Studies have found it to be extremely effective at removing impurities from the air.

GROW-LIKE-A-PRO TIP Extend your peace lily's bloom time by keeping water away from the flowers. If you mist the plant, put little plastic bags over the flowers before you spritz the leaves.

Cacti

*N*o collection of hardy houseplants would be complete without the cactus. The popular varieties I've selected are not only easy to grow—they flower too. You can buy them at almost any garden center.

Christmas Cactus

(Schlumbergera bridgesii)

Give this holiday bloomer bright light in summer and early fall, and you'll be rewarded with loads of winter flowers. The Christmas cactus has arched, pointy leaves that shoot out pretty buds in a variety of colors like pink, red, apricot, white, and other hues.

BASIC CARE Moderate light is best for this flowering plant, so make a home for your Christmas cactus in an east or west window. Though it's called a cactus, the schlumbergera acts more like an ordinary houseplant: It needs regular watering when the soil gets dry. So, check the soil at least once a week and water as needed. Water less from April through September, the Christmas cactus's dormant period. Once your plant starts to bloom, it will keep its flowers longer if you keep it in a cooler spot, away from any heating vents or warm drafts. To encourage the schlumbergera to bloom again next year, give it some time in the fall in a darker place with nighttime temps of 50 or 55 degrees. Ideally, keep your cactus in a room you don't use often (so it's dark in the evening). The Christmas cactus doesn't need much food; fertilize it about once a quarter or less.

GROW-LIKE-A-PRO TIP After your plant has finished blooming, it's time to prune. Cut or pinch back excess leaves at the joints. This will promote more buds for next year.

Cactus
(Cereus peruviana and *Rebutia)*

A perfect-for-beginners species, the column cactus (*Cereus peruviana*) thrives on negligence. Also called the Peruvian torch or Peruvian apple cactus, the column has that classic, tall, clublike shape that many people associate with these desert dwellers. If you're lucky (see tip below), it will bloom with large white, fragrant flowers in the spring. Another good starter cactus is the crown (*Rebutia*), which is pictured. Native to the Andes mountains, it looks like a giant green egg covered in fuzzy spines. In the spring and summer, crown cacti turnout bold flowers in red, orange, yellow, pink, or white, depending on the variety. As with any cactus, the key ingredients to success with this prickly pair are bright, warm sunlight and minimal water. Because these cacti are so adept at storing water, they can become heavy plants; choose a sturdy container that will anchor your cactus (a plastic pot is likely to tip over from the weight).

BASIC CARE Most cacti love a hot, sunny west or south window. But, being extra-adaptable, the column can even survive without a window! Cacti love the warm, dry conditions that exist in most homes during the colder months; no humidifiers needed here. Like most, these cacti are camels. You can go for months at a time during the winter without watering. Take an extended vacation, and they won't even know you're gone. But they do need a bit more H_2O when spring arrives, and they're getting ready to flower. Even then, let the soil get quite dry before you water. You can use the pencil test with cacti: Stick a pencil into the potting mix and then pull it out again. If you see any particles on the pencil, the soil's still moist; don't water just yet.

Fortunately, these low-care favorites also tell you when they're thirsty; their "skin" will appear wrinkled and shriveled when they really need a drink. You don't have to bother with fertilizer for most of the year; do feed your prickly pair a few times during the summer.

GROW-LIKE-A-PRO TIP For cacti to bloom, they need a rest in the late fall and winter. If you keep yours in a space that gets plenty of sun by day but turns quite cool at night (down to 50 degrees is fine) for about three months, you'll be rewarded with bold flowers in the spring.

Quick Reference

When a Plant's Past Its Prime

*i*f you pick up some of the plants in this book, you're bound to have healthy greenery for many years to come. Now that you can select plants with confidence, you could be at risk for developing "jungle house," where every shelf, sideboard, end table, or other vacant surface is covered with foliage. It's easy to get carried away and treat every bit of green—no matter what condition it's in—as something sacred.

Perhaps you have a plant that's been hanging in there for many years, but now looks downright mangy. If it doesn't respond to basic care, it's okay to say sayonara. Really. Don't feel guilty! Once a plant is detracting from your decor, rather than adding to it, and you're unable to revive the thing, it's time to let go. Think of it this way: The plant may have cost you $4.99 for ten years of soothing greenery. At $0.50 per year, that's one cost-effective investment!

For natural beauty that won't overwhelm your decor, select just a few striking specimens. Then, grow with the flow.

Photo Credits

Courtesy Cynthia McKenney: 31, 37, 39, 41, 43 45, 47, 49,
    51, 53, 55, 61, 65, 67, 69, 73, 75, 85
Courtesy Logee's Greenhouse: 59, 97, 105
Courtesy Monrovia: 35
Courtesy Top Tropicals: 57, 63, 71, 79, 81, 89, 95, 99, 101
Courtesy cfgphoto.com: 33, 77
Courtesy Paul S. Drobot: 83
Courtesy White Flower Farm: 91, 93

Acknowledgments

I would like to thank the plant and gardening experts who shared so much helpful information with me as I was researching this book.

I'm especially grateful to Ronald C. Smith, PhD, horticulturist at North Dakota State University's extension service, who offered such smart advice and interesting growing tips. Smith has been answering people's plant questions for years on the Hortiscope website at NDSU, and this site can help anyone with just about any plant-care problem (visit www.ext.nodak.edu/extnews/hortiscope/contents.htm and click on "Houseplants").

Special thanks to Mary Jo Bridge Palmer of Sam Bridge Nursery in Greenwich, Connecticut. Palmer is a walking, talking plant encyclopedia. She loves houseplants in particular and was kind enough to share some of her favorites with me.

Thanks also to Mary Jo Modica, professor of horticulture at the University of Alabama arboretum; Barbara Pierson, the nursery manager at White Flower Farm, for her advice on easy-care flowering plants; Toby Mancini, specialty grower at Monrovia in Visalia, California, and Cynthia McKenney, associate professor of horticulture at Texas A&M University. For an excellent database of houseplants, go to the Texas A&M site, aggie-horticulture.tamu.edu/interiorscape/index.html.

Thanks to my family for their encouragement. I learned about plants at the hands of my father, who filled our home with greenery of all shapes and sizes. He still calls on me to do the plant-sitting whenever the family goes on vacation. Though my mom claims to have a brown thumb, she has been a wonderful reader, editor, and cheerleader throughout this project. My aunt Anne has been an inspiration to me; I really admire her talent for gardening and her enthusiastic approach to life. I'm also so grateful to my sister, Margaret, who is always there for me—whether I need her help with proofreading or with personal matters. Finally, thanks to my husband, Tommy, for his love and support.

Index

African violet, 15, 18, 88–89
Air circulation, 16
Aloe vera (medicine plant), 6, 60–61
Amaryllis, 90–91
Arrowhead plant, 15, 18, 30–31
Baby's tears, 10, 32–33
Bathroom, plants in, 27
Beautiful-plant tips, 14–16
Brown ends/spots, 22–23
Bugs, 20–21
Cacti, 6, 103–108
Cast-iron plant, 6, 10, 19, 34–35
Century plant, 6, 36–37
Chinese evergreen, 10, 19, 38–39
Christmas cactus, 104–105
Clivia, 92–93
Corn plant, 6, 40–41
Cuttings, tip or leaf, 18–19
Dancing ladies, 94–95
Displaying plants, 25–27
    in bathroom, 27
    decorating containers, 27
    feng shui perspective, 26
    in groupings, 25–26
    in rock garden, 26
    in windows, 27
Disposing of plants, 109–110
Dividing plants, 18–19
Dracaenas, 6
Dumb Cane, 42–43
Dwarf schefflera, 10, 15, 44–45
English Ivy, 46–47
Fans, 16
Fatsia, 10, 15, 48–49
Fertilizer, 11–13

for lazy gardeners, 16
liquid, 12, 16
seafood, 13
sick plants and, 13
spikes, 12
Flowering plants, 87–101
    African violet, 15, 18, 88–89
    amaryllis, 90–91
    clivia, 92–93
    dancing ladies, 94–95
    geranium, 96–97
    kalanchoe, 98–99
    peace lily, 100–101
Foliage plants, 29–85
    arrowhead plant, 15, 18, 30–31
    baby's tears, 10, 32–33
    cast-iron plant, 6, 10, 19, 34–35
    century plant, 6, 36–37
    Chinese evergreen, 10, 19, 38–39
    corn plant, 6, 40–41
    dumb cane, 42–43
    dwarf schefflera, 10, 15, 44–45
    English Ivy, 46–47
    fatsia, 10, 15, 48–49
    heart ivy, 18, 50–51
    jade plant, 6, 15, 18, 26, 52–53
    Janet Craig, 6, 10, 19, 54–55
    kalanchoe, 15, 18
    lacy-tree philodendron, 56–57
    lady palm, 58–59
    medicine plant (aloe vera), 6, 60–61
    parlor palm, 10, 62–63
    ponytail palm, 6, 64–65
    pothos, 10, 18, 66–67
    prayer plant, 68–69

Foliage plants *cont'd*
    rosemary, 70–71
    rubber tree, 6, 10, 19, 72–73
    screw pine, 19, 74–75
    snake plant, 6, 19, 78–79
    southern yew, 6, 76–77
    spider plant, 80–81
    table fern, 82–83
    wandering jew, 18, 84–85
Food. *See* Fertilizer
Geranium, 96–97
Groupings, 25–26
Heart ivy, 10, 18, 50–51
Hints/tips, for beautiful plants, 14–16
Humidifiers, 15
HydraFeed, 16
Jade plant, 6, 15, 18, 26, 52–53
Janet Craig, 6, 10, 19, 54–55
Kalanchoe, 15, 18, 98–99
Lady palm, 58–59
Leaf cuttings, 18
Light, 1–3. *See also specific plants*
    geographical variations, 2–3
    low, plants loving, 10
    positioning plants and, 2
Medicine plant (aloe vera), 6, 60–61
Multiplying plants, 17–19
    cuttings, 18
    dividing plants, 18–19
Names, of plants, x. *See also specific
    names*
Parlor palm, 10, 62–63
Philodendron, lacy-tree, 56–57
Plant shine spray, 15
Ponytail palm, 6, 64–65
Pothos, 10, 18, 66–67
Potting plants, 7–9
    clay vs. plastic pots, 8
    freshening soil mix, 9
    repotting, 9, 23–24
    selecting pots, 7–8
    soil mix, 8

Prayer plant, 68–69
Problem solving, 20–24
    brown spots, 22–23
    bugs, 20–21
    disposal time, 109–110
    plants die after repotting, 23–24
    root analysis, 24
    tip burn, 22
Propagating plants. *See* Multiplying
plants
    Repotting, 9, 23–24
    Rock garden, 26
    Root analysis, 24
    Rosemary, 70–71
    Rubber tree, 6, 10, 19, 72–73
    Schefflera, 10, 15, 44–45
    Screw pine, 19, 74–75
    Shiny leaves, 15
    Sick plants
    healing. *See* Problem solving
    not feeding, 13
Snake plant, 6, 19, 78–79
Soil (potting mix), 8, 9
Southern yew, 6, 76–77
Spider plant, 80–81
Spray bottles, 16
Streptocarpella. *See* Dancing ladies
Sun. *See* Light
Table fern, 82–83
Tip burn, 22
Tip cuttings, 18
Troubleshooting. *See* Problem solving
Wandering jew, 18, 84–85
Water, 4–6
    determining need for, 5
    plants needing least, 6
    seasonal considerations, 5–6
    temperature, 6
Windows
    plant positions and, 2
    plants in, 27